Words for Things Left Unsaid

Words for Things Left Unsaid

by

Ethan Goffman

Cover design by Shay Culligan

ISBN: 978-1-950462-78-0

Kelsay Books Inc.

kelsaybooks.com

502 S 1040 E, A119
American Fork, Utah 84003

To Marianne, without whom there would be no poetry in my life.

The cycle of estrogen takes this small molecule through the bloodstream until it reaches cells such as uterine cells. An estrogen molecule has just transformed into a floating figure. She is attracted to the lotus flowers, which represent estrogen receptors on the surface of a cell. The flower captures her, and together they enter the cell and then the red cell nucleus. They then are bound to the purple DNA inside the nucleus. At this point, they cause the DNA to ultimately produce substances that cause the feelings and actions that estrogen is meant to trigger. Estrogen causes many, many things to occur.

Reference for description, "Biochemistry," Lubert Stryer, p. 1001, 1988.

Contents

Part 5. All You Need Is Love?

Part 6. The Riddle of Existence

Part 7. The Book of Thelma

Part 8. Inheritance Lost

Part 9. This Crazy, Wonderful, Dying Planet

Acknowledgments

The author gratefully acknowledges the following journals for publishing versions of these poems:

Blazevox: "A Reply to Richard Dawkins"
Burgeon: "Waiting to Cross a Busy Road"
Loch Raven Review: "To a Futon Couch"
Madness Muse: "Melania," "On Hearing that the Trump Administration Is Delaying Putting Harriet Tubman on the $20 Bill," "Out of Touch in Trump's America," "Proverb on Turtle's Back," "A Strange Dream," "A Thanksgiving Prayer"
Mad Swirl: "The Force Is Not with Me," "Precarious Is an Understatement," "Taxonomy of History"
Ramingo's Porch: "Eating Bitter Herbs," "To a Dead Cat"
Under the Bleachers: "The One Thing that Keeps Me from Having an Affair," "Tennis Scapegoat," "To Oblivion"
Setu: "Animals Are Our Friends," "Eight Million Years," "The End," "I Digress," "Insomnia," "It Must Be Hard to Be God," "Life Is Short and Death Is Long," "Thelma and the Blue Jay," "This House We Built," Vishnu Comes to Earth in the Form of a Cat"

And these anthologies:

Epiphanies of Love, Ed. Claudine Nash, 2019: "After the Concert"
The Music of the Aztecs, Ed. David Churchill, 2019: "The Force Is Not with Me," "Laughter Makes the World Go 'Round," "Taxonomy of History," "When My Wife Gave Birth."
Narwhal's Lament, Ed. Chani Zwibel, 2019: "A Hare's Breadth"

SPECIAL THANKS to Marianne Szlyk and John McDonald for patiently and thoughtfully critiquing the manuscript.

AND THANKS for their friendship, and for supporting my writing, to Lisa Goffman, Amy Goffman, Rachel Woolley, Eric Siegel, Karen Eilenberg, Stacie Marinelli, David Churchill, Michael Anthony Ingram, and Nancy Bain.

Part 1. A Brief Slog Through History

Good Morning Sinshine

A snake twists upon the gnarled bark
tying herself in knots;
naught can stop her naughty path.
She slithers stealthily, the silence of the snake
the sound of one reptile breathing
quieter than one hand clapping
the sound of silence
a cataclysm carefully calibrated.

She stretches toward sun
though it may burn her,
the glowing red orb
the circle of sin
the apple of alchemy.
The serpent circles herself
entwining with
a looping, leafy embroidery.

She is woman she is man
she is, briefly
the transcendent being
she yearns to be.

Eve creeps below
almost a snake herself
slithering
stealthy
low to the ground

ready for
the mating ritual
the entwined love
that will begin
history.

Love the snake
and all things that creep, crawl,
flutter and fly,
the slithering rope that fits so comfortably
within Eve's being.

This bite of apple
this flight too close to the sun
in 6,000 years
or 200,000
will be our doom.

Taxonomy of History

There are three main branches in the study of History:

The History of the Past
The History of What Happened
The History of What the Hell Happened!

The last, less respected than the others,
is sometimes known as *The History of One Damned Thing After
Another.*

There are three even less reputable branches of history:

The History of the Future
The History of What Might Have Happened
The History of What Never Happened

Most historians don't recognize these branches. Even some of the
more refined poets scorn them.

Still they are thunderstorms, pummeling fields of cantankerous,
yearning weeds
young weeds that sprout from drenched soil and spew outlaw
seeds.

To Oblivion

North is the opposite of south
yet also the same
if you go far enough
you get where you came.

We arrive at winter every year
the primeval frost
the frozen soul within us
and without.

Without us the planet still revolves
around itself
an infinite journey to oblivion.

Our own journey is much shorter.

Whether we face
nuclear winter
or climate change summer
how capable we humans are at finding
ways to destroy ourselves.

Fire and ice
Summer and winter
swallowing each other.
Yin is yang is yang is yin
Ping is pong is kong is king.

There are no opposites
Just a continuous line
North
to a blurring, frigid white.

The End

Life goes by so fast
before you know it you're long dead.

But how do you know it if you're dead?

I'd like to stick around to see how it all ends
for the poor perplexed human race
but don't want to take the trouble
to slog my way through
history's interminable march.

It would be nice to be an omni-consciousness
watching life like a movie
The grand sweep of it
The drama, the passion
the cast of billions!

I'd like to see if we destroy ourselves,
how we destroy ourselves.
Fire or ice.
Nuclear rain or slow climate boil.
Or a little of both, sweet and sour.

Perhaps we'll survive into unimaginable futures
spawn vast galactic empires
evolve beyond our imagination
become the omni-consciousness.

It would be nice to see it all,
but who wants to live it day by excruciating day?

Like a kid who can't stand to read through the whole goddamn
book
       I'd just like a peek at the ending, please.

Eve and Adam Look Down from Purgatory

Adam: Did people really go to the moon?

Eve: Physically they did, but spiritually not. Spiritually, the whole thing was a fake. We remain earthbound souls.

Adam: Is the Earth round or flat?

Eve: Flat. In eons past the Earth was round, but now it's an interminable gold coin on an obese, arthritic elephant's back jam-packed with angry mobs struggling to push each other off the edge.

Adam: Is there a God?

Eve: The truth is, people have been around for 6,000 years—or is it 200,000—and we still don't know. One thing's for certain, though. There is a Satan.

Adam: Isn't that just conjecture?

Eve: I've known it to be so ever since I ate the apple. People are unfair to snakes, though. We should love them and treat them kindly.

Adam: What will the weather be tomorrow?

Eve: Cloudy, with a chance of death.

Part 2. Out of Touch in Trump's America

A Strange Dream

I had a dream,
or read a science fiction book
or saw a movie

In which a black man
with a Muslim name
was President
of the United States

But that couldn't have actually happened, could it?

Melania

Seeing Melania Trump on TV the other day, I realized with a gasp
that she's beautiful. I'd never really noticed.
It's as if Princess Leia had married Jabba the Hut.

A Thanksgiving Prayer

We give thanks, O Lord
for the land we stole
        from its rightful inhabitants

Allowing us to dine
on this righteous feast
of indigestion.

Hillary Clinton

How do you stand it?
Called a witch, a wench, a whore,
probed, prodded, investigated,
then investigated more.

Liar, Cheater,
Madam, Pimp,
Child Molester.

They draw you
bloated and grotesque
stamp your face on toilet paper.

Like Helen of Troy,
the face that launched a thousand abuses,
a blonde façade hiding your
greying, thinning hair.

The witch hunt is on
and on and on.

They call you many names:
Jezebel.
Stalin.
Satan.
Hitler.

How do you stand it?
you, a frail, aging human being
with memory stuttering away in fragments

How do you stand it,
Donald Trump?

On Hearing that the Trump Administration Is Delaying Putting Harriet Tubman on the $20 Bill

As Martin Luther King, Jr. put it
Sometimes "wait" means "never."

What do they fear?
that Harriet will bleed monthly over all those fresh, green bills?
A bloody stain on our history?

To some, women are dirtier than money
dirtier than ripping
A bawling child from its terrified parents.

Out of Touch in Trump's America

My friends and I
clinging to part-time and temporary jobs
are so hopeless
that we don't even grope and harass women.
What a bunch of *losers* we are!

Proverb on Turtle's Back

We did not borrow this world from our children,
We stole it from the Native American ancestors.

Part 3. I Am an Embarrassment to Myself

The Force Is Not with Me

I am the guy in a red shirt in every episode of Star Trek
Who dies in the first scene or two.
I am not Spock.
I am not Kirk.
I am not the guest vixen in a low-cut blouse and mini-skirt.
I am Crew Member #3.

In our own minds we are all the hero
A colossus astride history,
Xena, Warrior Princess.

     * *

A wise man
who realized his true significance in the Great Script of Life
recently threw himself in front of the morning metro train.

I was late for work.
How thoughtless of him.

Tennis Scapegoat

I suck at tennis.
Diving for loose balls I plunk them clumsily against the net.

Springing forward to unleash my killer backhand,
I splotch the ball against the edge of my racket.
Miraculously, it wheezes over the net,
to the great glee of the slobbering giant
who waits on the other side
smashing a killer blow.

I suck at tennis.
Why do I keep at it?
when I could stay at home,
watching
the magnificent champions born to play the game
and remain
a safe distance from my ineptitude.

Isn't that the American way?
Hours upon days gawking at the dazzling professionals
dancing like angels across the court
while you slouch on a couch
growing a killer gut.

I suck at tennis;
I provide a useful service
heroic almost
to the weekend warriors
who can feel, just for an instant,
that they are part of a line of greatness
Borg, Navratilova, Federer, Serena
wielding their battle axes
striking another killer blow
against another hapless challenger.

There is no Hercules
without a hydra
no Beowulf
without a Grendel
no Rama
without a
demon king.
Villains are the deep heartbeat
of history and myth!

Still I most resemble
that shuffling goblin Gandalf kills without a glance
on his way to battle the Nazgul.

No one is a hero
without someone they can slay,
No champ without a chump.

I provide a useful service
as an extra
in a cast of thousands.

I am a tennis scapegoat. I exist for a reason.

Still on rare occasions I surprise.
Somehow my desperate lunge
sends the ball bouncing off the cord
careening to the other side at an angle
impossible to return.

For an instant I am a champion,
Game, set, and match!

A Fight With the Past

every day of my life
every morning every noon every evening every night
I am in a brutal fight
with the past

I cannot win
but on a good day
we can slug it out
to a draw

I can tumble into bed
bleeding but
still erect
on my path to
insomnia

Day after day
deploying the rope-a-dope
(after all one cannot face the past directly
without being instantly knocked on one's ass)
I feel like Muhammed Ali
sting like a butterfly, float like a bee

like the aging Ali I have been
battered into
a sickness of the brain
leaving me
staggered, stuttering
incoherent

I cannot speak
my truth
I have lost who I am
who I might have hoped to be
who I never was

you cannot beat the past
even before you are born
the past has already
won

Laughter Makes the World Go 'Round

I can't spread love
because I just don't have enough,
but I'd love to spread laughter
carry it like cash
spilling from my pockets,

hand it out to strangers, friends, colleagues,
even enemies
as tips
as advice
as succulent nibbles.

Laughter is double edged.
Anger is its father
a blade that slices
leaving raw wounds in tender flesh.

Anger is those wounds
and salt in those wounds
and venom in that salt.

So I won't spread anger
and I can't spread love,
I'm no cupid with a quiver full of arrows;
my love quiver is straight out empty.

What arrows I do have are more ambiguous
with spikes and perforated edges;
I'd love to shoot them about randomly
aiming straight and true.

Laughter in my quiver
laughter in my pocket
an ointment rich and creamy
cool and invigorating,
a salve that transmutes
water into wine
pigshit into gold.

all the anger and bitterness in the world transformed into
an arrow tip, a sticky barbed mass that twists itself
straight into the bleeding gut
yet somehow heals.

Part 4. Paradoxes and Mind Benders

Difficult and Impossible Problems: SOLVED!

It's easy to solve the Rubik's Cube
You just need six colors of paint
and six paintbrushes.

A tree falling in a forest
hasn't really fallen
until someone comes across it
in which case it has.

Who can't square the circle?
Just take four equidistance points
and pull them out till they form sharp edges
Voila, a square!

An unstoppable force
will simply pass through an immovable object
leaving both unharmed.

It's easy to bring about world peace
we just need to fire off a few thousand nuclear warheads
Voila! The peace of the grave.

this last is the only problem
humanity is actually capable of solving.

I know I can't solve the god-damned Rubik's Cube!

The Mind-Body Problem: SOLVED!

The body is an embarrassment
a mess of ill-fitting shapes strewn together
with gangly protrusions and strange orifices.

The body imprisons us
leaves us yearning for air every few seconds, water every few
       hours,
masticated organic matter
       over and over and over and over.

The body forces us to
       gush stinky substances
so that periodically
       we must hide ourselves away.

It's disgusting!

I have the solution!
Let's get rid of our bodies

and exist as pure aetherial beings.

No time for excuses
Let's do it!

The Abortion Controversy: SOLVED!

It is cruel and unusual
to allow a baby to be born
into a world
where it will suffer
pain and humiliation
failure and sorrow
and finally
death.

Every baby should have to sign
a certificate of agreement
before being born.

But it's a metaphysical impossibility.

The alternative,
abortion,
is just as cruel.
A denial of thought
aspiration
hope,
the destruction
of a unique person.
A denial
of such carnal enjoyments
as hamburgers
and ice cream
(which, however,
deny other sentient beings
their inalienable rights
to the products of their own bodies,
to their lives.)

The only solution
is mass sterilization.

With no humans
the Earth would be green and blue, swirling with life
verdant
and beautiful.

I Digress

People tell me I digress too much
like the time I was on the phone with my sister
talking about how humans acquire
the miracle of speech, which she studies,
she runs a research lab at Purdue University,
which is kind of amazing considering
she started off life aimless, going nowhere
which happens to many of us, after all
how do we decide what to do in this
vast and complex world
bewildering
it is wildering, wide and wild
with biodiversity, lush with crazy beasts
like sloths, how do they spend their lives
hanging upside down
doesn't the blood rush to their heads?
although the world is so confusing maybe we'd all be better off
hanging upside down, trying to connect the strands
of experience, of light, of vision
like paint whipped at random from the brush of
an insane abstract expressionist,
is that art, my child could do that?
but children are geniuses in a way
insane little geniuses
mad scientists cooking up trouble
cooking up batches of fresh
dream cookies lush with chocolate
mmmmmmmmmmmmmmmm, chocolate, invented by the Aztecs
whom we colonists discovered
and destroyed in our mad wanderings around
this crazy, mixed-up globe,
we are all colonists, in a way
wandering the world conquering
other species, other tribes

raping and slaughtering
stealing from their cultures to make something
new and old and beautiful
gorgeous and terrible
intricate and random
that's the way the world works, infinite strands
flung and mixed and recombined.
Chaos!
Order!

So you see
I have not been digressing after all.

Total Eclipse

Annie Dillard writes of how a total eclipse
spells out infinity
Shows humans our place in the cosmos
Our mortality
Our utter dependence on natural forces
that don't just dwarf us, they mosquito us
don't just mosquito us, they bacteria us.
Fill us with awe.
Totality.

But I say
What's the big deal?
It gets dark every night anyway
when the Earth below us blocks out the sun.

I'm wise to your writerly tricks, Annie.
You were just looking for a subject.
That's what writers do.
A total eclipse doesn't tell us anything
we shouldn't know anyway
if we're the least bit wise
to nature's everyday wonders.

Part 5. All You Need Is Love?

to a futon couch

you lie there
i lie on you
nibbling poems
tidbits of truth
in the form of lies

the evening slips away
me
slouched
on a futon couch

snapped upright
in theory at least

in reality
somehow askew
mattress straining to slide off
unsure what it's doing here
why it exists

above floats
a mystery disc
the Earth
a half dome lighting late hours

**

i peek at the
blue and white swirl
the southern hemisphere

gaze north north north
boring through
water soil rock magma

focus on
the u. s. of a.
zoom in on
maryland
on
this town, this small house, this room, this futon couch
on
myself contemplating worlds

Above planets swirl;
a fan whispers me a cooling breeze

sweet company as I enter the realm
of poesy and dreams from around
this churning yearning sphere

**

i visit this futon couch
this room
this universe
every evening
lights dimmed

under doctor's orders
to cure my insomnia
a slow calming before
the final plunge

into the universe of self
of nothingness

i visit nightly
this obscure room

long the realm of an occasional guest
a cat briefly escaping its people

no stars wink
on the great ceiling
only blankness

once
we had planned
to strew suns comets galaxies
to keep watch upon the night

to be gazed at
to spread wonder and whimsy

in this small room we had built
for the child we never had

When My Wife Gave Birth

When my wife gave birth,
she gave birth to cats,
a feisty calico
and a tabby
who purred so loud
it about shook the world.

I said, Isn't something the matter?
Don't most women
give birth to human babies
and not cats?

She threw me a look
half glance, half glare
as if to say
What more did you expect,
you who could never give birth to anything?

In all likelihood
my wife and I will survive our children
leaving us lonely and alone
to live out our days.

The One Thing that Keeps Me from Having an Affair. . .

is that it would violate everything I believe in
and bring great suffering to those I love
and shame upon myself.

Still James Bond,
Bill Clinton and
others of their ilk
had a point.
Why not sleep with a thousand beautiful women?
experience what they have to offer
learn the crannies and rhythms of their bodies
the musky smells
their moods and shifting dreams
the intimate details of their homes their jewelry
the deodorants and perfumes that infuse their skin
mingled with sweet-and-sour sweat.

Why not
learn the intimate histories of a thousand cultures
experience ten thousand flavors
tarragon, wild mint, jalapeno, cardamom, ginger, salt and pepper
Kenyan, Salvadoran, Balinese, Inuit, Narnian
(Tiger Woods was boring,
blonde after blonde after blonde after blonde).

Why not
mingle intimately with all the world
and beyond.

Of course, I'm no Bond.
If I did attempt to stray
I would just humiliate myself.

Best to stick with the familiar and true
it takes a lifetime and more to know.

This House We Built

This house we built:
a man a woman and two cats
the perfect family just as God intended.

This house that built us:
foundation miles thick
picture window streaming with life
yellow shingles and orange fence
blazing with light.

This house the contractors built
for cash
although with
a certain pride
perhaps even
love
that they were making something lasting
to bind the universe in its small way.

Is it love that builds things?
Or is it cement, nails, wood, and plaster?
Or is it money?

This house we had built
or that always existed
surrounded by birdsong in the trees we planted
by scampering squirrels
by rabbits feasting
on the tall fescue.

This house made of commerce
made of love.

This house we built,
a man a woman and two cats
the perfect family just as God intended.

So unlike
two men and a baby
a man a woman two dogs and a gerbil
a woman a child a goldfish
abominations all

unless they are built
with love and kindness.

Part 6. The Riddle of Existence

Precarious Is an Understatement

I am perched
atop a knife edge
balanced on a dead
tree trunk
on the lip of a volcano
suspended on a sheet of melting ice
floating on an ocean boiling with rage
itself in a miniscule depression
on a vast turtle's back.
The turtle is
flapping its tiny flippers
desperately trying to cross
an ethereal nothingness
punctuated by wisps of mist.

There cannot be wisps in nothingness.

All of this is an illusion
conceived in the mind of a monarch butterfly
radiant with hope
or with love
or with nihilism
on the edge of extinction
perched on my nose
tickling
like a universe of feathers.

I remain teetering on the knife edge
as it cuts into the sole of my foot,
the fate of my soul
floating in
the misty, empty air.

A Reply to Richard Dawkins

I refute it thus.
—Samuel Johnson, kicking a stone to refute Bishop Berkeley's theory of the
   nonexistence of matter.

Perhaps we are
automatons
that exist only to survive and breed
spewing out
new generations.

Perhaps personality, individuality, consciousness,
is just an accident
a flickering illusion emanating from a collection of impulses
only seeming to cohere.

If you sever one part of the brain
You are not the same person.
You lose speech, memory, the ability to reason.
You are an exquisite corpse.
You are garble.
You are you yet not you.

Perhaps the brain is just a collection of impulses
a sophisticated computer that has made us
the most successful species on this planet,

at least until we finish our collective suicide

obliterating wondrous multitudes along with ourselves
redwoods and black bears, bees and spiders
fungi and sloths, eagles and robins and worms, aardvarks and ants;
the delicate web of life that we are part of
yet act apart from.

We are the uber species, killing us softly.

Monty Python had it right
the search for meaning is a kind of joke.

Not even a cosmic joke,
but a minor giggle.

a hiccup that can't be terrified or drowned away
a byproduct of the struggle to
breed.

a spirit,
a source of pure love, rubs against me and purrs

Are We Poems?

The story is writing you
you are not writing the story.
The poem is your life
your life is not a poem.

Your life is many poems
perhaps an epic
of a wily adventurer,

perhaps a sonnet
of a doomed love affair
a sun quickly setting.

Perhaps a poet is writing this
perhaps a failed comic
is stuttering it on a grand stage
as tomatoes rain down.

This poem is not being written
this poem is writing the world.

This world is only stories
this world is only dreams
an intricate bouquet of
milkweed, chicory, spear thistle

that words strain to capture
flickering ghosts on a video screen.

Without writers there is no world
without a world no writers.

This world is flitting
ephemeral
always on the edge of
vanishing.

This world is eternal
it will outlive us all
all of us who create it.

It Must Be Hard to Be God

Here's the dilemma. You could create a world of beauty and
harmony
angels strumming gorgeous harps, incandescent melodies,
perfection itself.
Perfectly boring.

Music is beauty plus dissonance.
Heavenly music is beauty without dissonance.
The Talking Heads sang, "heaven is a place where nothing ever
happens."
William Blake wrote, "Milton is of the devil's own party."

Satan is the mother of invention.
Satan animates.

Satan sucks! Auschwitz is just one fragment in a vast mosaic of
suffering.
The atheists are right. The universe is too cruel for any creator.

The atheists are wrong. The universe cannot exist without moral
order.

If there is a god, I curse Him to high heaven
and to the depths of hell!

Imagine a world with only minor pains.
Instead of fire and ice
its history would culminate in
a civil debate with little insults
and paper airplanes
hurled hither and yon,
and final reconciliation a group hug.

No Evangelical fire and fury.
The Book of Revelations as reimagined by Unitarians.
A far worse fate is hurtling toward us all.

I can never forgive God.
And if there is no God
I can never forgive
the vast, empty universe.

I curse the universe.
The universe doesn't answer.

Life Is Short and Death Is Long

We are all heading together into the same future
And that is death.
We are sisters and brothers in death.

All of life is a preparation for death
as some wise guy said ages ago.
Some wise guy now long dead.

Is death
A figure shrouded in a cloak
Swinging an enormous scythe that screams like a thousand winds
Reaping souls, grains of wheat in an endless field?

Perhaps death is a kindly fellow
nuzzling your cheek
As you pass through
a tunnel of radiant light
The opening of the doors of perception
Love itself.

Or death is
Nothing.

One can't imagine nothingness, since even the thought of
nothing is something
One can't imagine death although we know it's coming.

so perhaps it's best to live right
treat others kindly
and die with an easy mind.

Part 7. The Book of Thelma

Vishnu Comes to Earth in the Form of a Cat

Vishnu, protector and preserver of the universe,
came to Earth as a human,
Rama,
to end the dominion of the brutal demon, Ravana
and usher in 10,000 years of peace, light and happiness.

In a far more obscure matter,
Vishnu, great and mighty protector and preserver,
came to Earth as a cat,
Thelma,
to end my loneliness
and usher in 10 years of peace, light and happiness.

Thelma,
Mother Earth goddess,
queen of fertility,
womb sacrificed,
claws ripped away,
wild nature shorn.
That's the way it is with Earth goddesses.
They sacrifice something of themselves and a bountiful planet
springs forth.

Thelma
Empress of the universe
unique
though one of billions,
cycling through lives.
flitting ephemeral
Eternal Thelma.

Thelma and the Blue Jay

Our cat Thelma
at the big picture window
staring at a blue jay
bright, plumed, and perfect
as lovely and alive
as any unclothed work of art
in the Louvre.

Thelma crouches tensed, every iota alert.
Like a teenage boy gaping at pornography
on the picture window of the internet,
she gets to watch
but never gets to
pounce!

Triumphant Joy

Thelma, my love

I felt a strange
triumphant joy

When I grabbed you
stuffed your squirming body
into the cat carrier
zipped it up tight
as you writhed.

Was it the same
sensation
a hunter feels bringing down a deer
bounding through the forest?

The same
sensation
a cop feels
when he shoots the bad guy
27 times?

The urge
to conquer
The victorious instant
that I,
Judas Iscariot Goffman,
felt
as I brought down
my love and companion.

Perhaps this is hyperbole.

No, certainly it is.

77

Still for that instant
I felt
a universal instinct
or should I say extinct

a moment
of pure
triumphant joy.

To a Dead Cat

Your body lay crushed and broken
in the street
one eyeball bulging out, floating atop a crimson crest.

In life you had been
sleek and black
a fleeting shadow
glimpsed from the window.

I called animal control
to come pick up your broken body
the remnant that had been you.

I asked about a catch, spay, release program
to help the neighborhood's surviving strays
lucky enough to have so far evaded
their worst natural enemy
Cars
killers of the ecosphere and of small animals.

One of them got you good
Killed you dead
Hit and run.

In life you were sleek and black
a ruthless killer
scourge of birds, rabbits, voles
a mass murderer
an invasive species
black and sleek and beautiful
natural born killer
        and athlete
with moves beyond
        Michael Jordan.

Thelma will no longer tense suddenly
spring to the window
glare intensely at
her wild biological twin.

I stroke Thelma under her chin
her purring shakes the air, shakes my heart.
"you're lucky," I tell her.

I would kiss her furry head,
but I don't want a mouth full of cat hair.

In my dream that night
a dead eye stares up at me
floating atop a crescent crust of red.

Eight Million Years

Yowling and whining,
Callie and Thelma demand
breakfast each morning
walking over us
with imperious impunity.

Cats are
an astonishingly patient species.
They waited 8 million years,
hunting, breeding, dying, hunting
for their humans to appear on Earth.

They waited 8 million years
to evolve in the blink of an eye
from hunters to lovers
purring, rubbing, frolicking
ending the suffering of
all the lonely people,
becoming stars of stage and screen
of a billion videos.

They waited 8 million years
to become an invasive species
slaughtering birds and voles
and rare protected critters
in nooks and crannies of the globe
where no cat had ever been.

Our cats haunt us daily
ghosts of devastation future
ethereal angels of love.
We cannot live without them
as we hurl toward our common fate.

Part 8. Inheritance Lost

Eating Bitter Herbs

I used to slather horseradish on top of my matzo
as thick as possible
at our annual Passover dinner
the last remnant of a Judaism my parents had left behind
and I have abandoned altogether.

Once in a great while
I receive a message from an old friend or enemy
I have abandoned altogether
or who has abandoned me
asking for reconciliation.

I always tell them no,
I am a bitter man
the past is dead.

Why reawaken
feelings long gone.

Jesus might forgive
but I do not.

I love horseradish
slathered thick and zesty
a million little stings dancing on my tongue
tingles of life.

The sting of betrayal
is far more bitter.

The Hanging Tree of Life

after a photo in the Portraits of Life exhibit of Holocaust survivors, Montgomery College, September 2018

An impish grin
Like a favorite aunt I never had
a source of life
wherever she may live.

Her survival a fluke?

A picture of American vitality
in a stately Bethesda house
face floating above history.

She would spread brightness in any time or place.

At five, they ripped her father from her and sent him to Auschwitz;
she escaped to Italy.

She is the aunt I never had
my own family history ripped of leaves and branches
and of roots.

She lived the American dream
a sage, a scholar
a founding mother
an Atlas
shouldering the burden of her community.

She must have
brought light to many parties
nibbled on
fine hors d'oeuvres
petit fours, guacamole, sushi
sipped on
champagne, Sake
spilling from the American horn of plenty
a multicultural wonder, *e pluribus unum*
from many one cuisine.

She must have
laughed and chatted
quipped about the latest political scandal
each small victory in the fight for women's rights
celebrating a life that once dangled on
a thread of dust.

She urges us
not to give in to hate
to work together for a better world.

It's so easy for her to preach love
what does she have to fear
with her picture-perfect Bethesda existence
a literary star amid a social whirl?

How could she not succumb
to the hole ripped in her soul at five
how could hatred
not poison her heart her lungs her guts her bowels?

Over long years
she must have had uncountable nights of despair
her husband gone
her children fled their comfy nest
the dog
put down in an errand of mercy.

How could ugly thoughts not flock to her
thick flights of bats
shrieking that we all are victims
of our defective humanity.

We hate each other so
kill off leaf branch and root of our own tree.

What does it take to survive and plant anew
tend and water, let new roots sprout and sprawl
a thousand branches spring
ten thousand blossoms peek
from the bloody soil of hanging trees?

The Holocaust didn't occur in Germany
nor in eastern Europe
but on every corner
of the planet
most of all in the human soul

on the sacred ground
where each of us lives.

There is no story of a community that is not a story of barbarism
that friendly oak, that neighborhood tabby, that mother's voice
calling, laughing, to her children,
inhabit
a site of blood
where another tribe once lived.

Insomnia

I have been betrayed
by my family, my country
by friends, colleagues, acquaintances
by the ideal of democracy
by the courts, by checks and balances
by the gods, by God
by atheism
by agnosticism
by gnawing doubt
by arrogant certainty
by myself.

My wife lies beside me
peacefully asleep.
We touch
yet there is a strange distance between us.
At my feet,
always with me,
blazing with life,
the eternal Thelma.

Part 9. This Crazy, Wonderful, Dying Planet

After the Concert

Fireflies light up and vanish, strewing patterns
more gorgeous than our neighbor's Christmas lights display.
She is lighting up the night to show off.
They are lighting up the night
to continue as a species.

A bullfrog chorus thrums
in great bass patterns
through the sticky night air
pumping out music
thrumping out "we must endure"!

E.O. Wilson would be proud
of the thronging life
on display.
Our planet is not dead yet.

In the distance
a scattering of lanterns through the thick trees
lights up the curving path
in a lovely dance with nature
centering a picture
the art of human symmetry and the primal darkness
completing each other.

A cosmic harmony
behind the great hall's curving stone pillars
after the concert.

The electronic dazzle
of the music
lingers
in the sinews of our being,
we had sought it out, thrilled to it.

Yet this little scene,
this remnant of nature's grace
that we chanced upon
sneaking away from the crowd

completes the night.

A Hare's Breadth

One spring morning, pulling weeds
I glance up
at the fat brown bunny
grazing lazily on our untrimmed grass.
She pauses, as if to say,
"What, salad again for breakfast?"

A rabbit is just a machine, some scientists say
only slightly more advanced than a Roomba
designed for devouring grass
and spawning legions of bunnies.

I prefer to think she has a soul
though her one eye turned toward me
seems blank.
Is she aware of me
as a conscious being?

In any case, she is my long lost kin
from 65 million years ago
when our common foremother,
hairy, warm blooded
and quivering,
somehow escaped the fate
of the dinosaurs.

I've seen this rabbit before.
Almost every day
she's nibbling on the grass.
Our yard, I think, is her entire world.

She's lost her fear of humans,
lets me get within a hare's breadth
before I back away.

But something's startled her,
a premonition, perhaps?
I glance up again to see her bounding
to some other yard, some other world.

Waiting to Cross a Busy Road

I am trying to cross a busy road
at a spot with no crosswalk for miles and miles and miles and
miles
but someone must have constructed a machine of infinite car
generation
way down the road, due north, just past the horizon.
And another such machine due south.
That's the only explanation
for why the cars just kept coming and
coming and coming and coming and coming and coming and
imoc dna gnimoc dna gnimoc dna gnimoc dna gnimoc dna gnimoc

Wait, there's another possibility!
People could have constructed roads all over the planet
and hundreds of millions of cars to fill them.

Of course, that would be insane,
        a form of mass suicide,
over the short time horizon that is human existence.
The ecosphere couldn't survive
        the snaking, strangling network of roads and super-
        highways
the foulness spewing from tailpipes
        numberless as the stars
Relentless zooming vehicles making road kill of
ants flies beetles spiders snails turtles snakes voles mice rats
squirrels chipmunks skunks opossums deer elk wolves coyotes bear
and occasionally people

There's a third possibility.
Maybe the road ends just over the horizon
       in each direction
and loops back upon itself
so that a limited number of cars are traveling the same road over
and over and over
giving the illusion of infinitude
like an old Hollywood film where the camera pans over the same
set of performers
so they seem like massive crowds.

That must be it!
The least implausible explanation.

You might think I'm writing this from the safety of my home
emotion recollected in tranquility.
But it's scrawled in blood from my finger tips
pricked by thorns from a withered roadside locust tree.

I Apologize to the Animals

I apologize to the animals
original citizens
of this glistening orb.

I apologize
for how we have
slaughtered you
strangled you in nets of highways
leveled the trees that shelter you
poisoned your air and water,
fouling our own nest.

I apologize
that we have
bred and fattened you
pumped you up with hormones and antibiotics
crammed you into tiny cages
to make a quick meal,
fast bucks and fast food.

I am far from the worst offender
yet over a lifetime
I have feasted on scores of your relatives
strewn my own trail of waste and gluttony.

Noah, the legend goes, saved two of every animal.
We humans, the legend goes, took care of nature, restored the
Earth
when it was most needed.
A big lie.

We are more like guards at Auschwitz
marching species, two by two
to oblivion.

We have wounded Mother Earth
and our own souls.

You animals have always taken care of us
fed, clothed, sheltered us,
nourished our souls.

Now we need you most.
Yet we are killing you.

So I apologize

to
the great blue whale
and the tiny mite,
to cats and dogs, mewling and yipping in human-engineered
hordes
to cows and pigs
and chicks and geese and ducks all a-scurry
to the wily coyote and the mischievous rabbit
the pulsating heart of folklore and cartoons
to spiders floating above the earth
and giant tube worms blundering through the ocean's sunless
depths
to swarming military ants
and bees impregnating
flowers
and termites undermining the foundations
of countless houses
to dragonflies skimming lakes
and the eagle soaring overhead

to the earthworm crawling below
and the robin that eats and is eaten
to all the great chain of being.
Though it won't do a lick of good
what else can I do?
I apologize

Animals Are Our Friends

A deer stood by the side of the road
and gazed at me with querying eyes.

Deer no longer bolt at the sight of humans.
Although we are alien species,
we are kin.

Deer are taking over the suburbs
as peace-loving neighbors
who only want to eat our yards
our tomatoes and squash
an occasional flower.

A squirrel scampers visible for an instant.
Some force animated it, gave it life.
The same force that animates me
and my loved ones
and my enemies.

The fat brown rabbit
that inhabited our yard
has disappeared.
So has the earlier occupant,
a fierce hunter
who kept the birds as sparse
as the hairs on my aging head.

Layers and currents of history reside in our yard
an ocean of life
swelling with music.

It is not whales singing
but their distant cousins
sparrows, robins, crows
—the usual suspects—
a cardinal redder than blood
a jay blue as the sky
who pops by
as an occasional surprise
like a friend one hasn't seen in ages.

This is our home
all our homes.
It resides in our bones
and we in its soil
and primordial rocks.

yet we are also visitors
migrants

who will one day
be swept aside

and this small house overgrown with weeds.

About the Author

Ethan Goffman is an environmental and transit writer in Rockville, Maryland and a part-time teacher at Montgomery College. His non-fiction has appeared in *E: The Environmental Magazine, EarthTalk, Grist, The Progressive, Greater Greater Washington, the Baltimore Sun, Mobility Lab, The SSPP Blog,* and elsewhere. He is co-founder of It Takes a Community, a Montgomery College initiative that brings poetry to both students and local residents. In addition, Ethan is the founder and producer of the Poetry & Planet podcast on EarthTalk.org.

Made in the USA
Middletown, DE
15 February 2021